Colors
for
Living

Bedrooms

BY JENNIE L. PUGH WITH SANDRA RAGAN

ROCKPORT

First published in the United States of America by:
Rockport Publishers, Inc.
33 Commercial Street
Gloucester, MA 01930
Telephone: (978) 282-9590
Fax: (978) 283-2742

ISBN 1-56496-550-3

2 4 6 8 10 9 7 5 3

Art Director: Lynne Havighurst
Production: Sara Day Graphic Design
Cover Photograph: © John M. Hall

Printed in china

Colors
for
Living

Bedrooms

GLOUCESTER MASSACHUSETTS

ROCKPORT PUBLISHERS

Photo: Eric Roth
Design: Joseph W. Drohan Associates

Dedicated to my mother,
who taught me to dream in color.

TABLE OF CONTENTS

PREFACE 8

COLOR ISN'T WHAT IT USED TO BE 12

CHOOSING THE BASE COLORS FOR YOUR PALETTE 14
COLOR AND FORM, COLOR AND FUNCTION, COLOR AND STYLE

THE NUTS AND BOLTS OF COLOR 20
THE COLOR WHEEL, COLOR THEORY

PURE COLORS 26
COLORS WITH INTENSITY

Cherry Red, Sunshine Yellow, Royal Blue, Purple, Orange Pepper, Emerald Green

TINTED COLORS 38
COLORS FOR TRANQUILITY

Rosy Pink, Mint Green, Conch Pink, Light Yellow, Cerulean Blue, Spring Lavender

SHADED COLORS 56
COLORS THAT COMFORT

Chinese Red, Deep Blue, Deep Gold, Burnt Orange, Aubergine, Ocher Green

MUTED COLORS 72
COLORS FOR EASY LIVING

Twilight Blue, Antique Rose, Willow Green, Dusky Peach, Harvest Grape, Copper Oxide Green

NEUTRAL COLORS 86
COLORS OF THE EARTH

Gunmetal Gray, Putty, Brown Cinnamon, Soft Camel, Bone White, Ebony

ELECTRIC COLORS 104
COLORS WITH ENERGY

Moroccan Red, Sunburst Yellow, Hot Plum, Ocean Blue, Persimmon Orange, Bright Chartreuse, Sizzle Pink

COLOR SWATCHES 114

COLOR GLOSSARY 122

INDEX 124

DIRECTORY OF PHOTOGRAPHERS 125

DIRECTORY OF ARCHITECTS, DESIGNERS, AND MANUFACTURERS 126

BIBLIOGRAPHY 127

Photo Credit: Bedroom by B&B Italia

The clear yellow of sunshine combined with natural bamboo pulls the seascape into this bedroom.

PREFACE

I have a love affair with the ocean. Not just any ocean—the western Caribbean. The colors there are the pale lavenders and hot tangerines of the sunrises and sunsets upon the water. The blues range from the turquoise of the shallows to the wine-dark blue of the deep water and night sky. Creamy sand beaches display shells of delicate pinks and corals.

For three years my husband and I sailed from the Chesapeake Bay to Honduras in a thirty-three-foot catamaran. Our bedroom was the forward cabin perched up over the pontoons. Each morning I woke face to face with the sea. Each day was a different color and a different mood.

For a time we rented a little house located in a fishing village in southern Belize. It was painted pale pink with white trim, and perched up on stilts thirty feet from the ocean's edge.

My fondest memories are of rising there at first light. From the bedroom window I looked out over the bay and saw the pale blue-gray sky streaked with yellow. The early morning sun soon became white. It slanted through the palms and made moving sparkles of light on the sand floor. High noon was yellow heat. It made the water a dark glare with diamonds jumping and bubbling. Time to rest inside, listen to the melodious birds, and cook the evening meal.

A *bedroom chaise is surrounded by the soft, gentle whisper of palest peach.*

After the heat of the sun broke in the afternoon, the shadows turned to a blue, then purple, haze. When the pink rays of the evening sun deepened to hot red and purple, people quietly wandered to the water's edge—to watch the sunlight blending with the kinetic energy of the sea. As the last of the deep purple faded, the sky and the sea became the same color.

Now we are back at home in the United States. We love living in the big city with our work and our friends. But we miss the serenity of living with nature day to day.

To keep alive our memories of sailing from island to island, the colors of the western Caribbean infuse our home. The living room is the color of early morning light, and the den is late sunset.

The bedroom is our sanctuary, a place to go at the end of a busy day to rest and renew. The colors are those of the reef. I literally took a conch shell to my painter, and now the walls are the soft, pale coral color of the inner spirals of a shell.

Tailored, crisp white canvas Roman-style shades are reminiscent of sails. The focal point of the room is a vintage vanity painted with a trompe l'oeil reef.

When you design your own bedroom, use the colors and images that make you feel good. After all, bedrooms are very personal and private spaces. Yours should be every bit as unique as you are.

Bedrooms have become daring, with a full spectrum of color applied in new and exciting ways.

COLOR ISN'T WHAT IT USED TO BE

Selecting a color palette for your bedroom can be quite a dilemma. A few hundred years ago, people had no such problem. The colors used in decoration came from natural dyes or pigments. The colors used to adorn sleeping areas were dictated by cultural traditions and folkways.

With the industrial age came the widespread availability of colorful fabrics and paints. Rich and exotic colors were no longer the exclusive domain of royalty; they could be part of everyone's world. The bedroom could be adorned according to individual tastes, although climate and tradition continued to dictate its style.

Today, in the age of information and communication, the challenge is dealing with excess. Our daily period of visual stimulation has expanded from eight to sixteen hours. We are bombarded with color in all sorts of advertising, neon signs, attention-grabbing mail, splashy decors, and television. Our color perception is so heightened that we can distinguish among thousands of colors.

Dyes, pigments, fabrics, paints, furniture, and art from every point of the globe are widely available and easy to obtain. With synthetic fibers and materials, designs from the wildest realms of imagination can be brought to life. All of these ingredients can be mixed and interpreted in infinite design styles.

Infinite design style is a very exciting prospect. This book was created to help you figure out where to begin and how to develop an integrated look. Take inspiration from the designs shown, then adapt them to suit your lifestyle and color preferences. Cut out the color swatches in the back of the book and use them as a foundation for designs of your own.

Like all good design, good bedroom design begins with a good concept. The equation for a focused concept includes:

- *Form:* the size and shape of the bedroom and furniture.
- *Function:* the ways the room is used by the people living there.
- *Style:* the ambiance of the space, created by the use of design elements such as furniture, furnishings, materials, art, and lighting.

Throughout the considerations of form, function, and style, you will weave color. And remember, the texture of a fabric, wall treatment, or floor—and the type of light in the room—can enhance or change the colors you choose.

Photo: Bedroom by Dakota Jackson

The owner's passion for collecting all kinds of artwork is reflected in this colorful contemporary bedroom.

CHOOSING THE BASE COLORS FOR YOUR PALETTE

There are as many ways of approaching the color palette as there are designs themselves. You can pull pictures out of magazines or recall an impression of a bedroom you have admired. Start with a beautiful Persian rug or a vintage quilt, or simply begin with your favorite color.

Some of the most successful bedroom color themes are based on interests and hobbies of the occupants. Someone who enjoys gardening might choose floral prints, people who are passionate about sailing might surround themselves with the blue hues of water. Colors can be selected to create the illusions of bygone eras or exotic faraway places.

When designing a bedroom, consider your own energy level and how much energy you would like in the atmosphere of the room: warm, intense hues of yellow and red will make the room vibrant; cool tints or shades of blue and green will create a more relaxed atmosphere.

A particular design challenge arises when two people share a bedroom. One may want a traditionally feminine bedroom color—such as pink—while the other may want a more masculine, "outdoors"-inspired color scheme. If you are careful in your choice of colors a successful compromise can be achieved most of the time. Experiment with tints of coral rather than pink, for an atmosphere that has the calming, tranquil effects of pink, but is not as directly associated with femininity. Finishing out the scheme with neutral-colored furnishings in bold, clean shapes will further diminish the boudoir image, and will make the surroundings feel more "natural."

When making color selections, consider the existing furniture styles and color schemes in other rooms of the house. Although it is not necessary to use the same colors in every area, the palettes of the rooms should work together for a smooth, visual transition between one space and another. A simple way to ensure this cohesiveness is to incorporate a single common color into all the schemes.

A good color scheme creates atmosphere in a bedroom; here, the combination of dark green and red suggest a rather formal European hunting lodge.

Photo: Bedroom by Baker Furniture

COLOR AND FORM

What we perceive as space and size is largely based on what we expect to see. So, the illusion of size or shape in a bedroom can be manipulated by altering the colors of the walls and ceiling. For instance, you can make one area look larger than another by painting it a lighter color. Shading wall-color with gray has a similar effect—making the shaded area appear more distant.

Cool colors appear to recede, adding depth to a room. Warm colors seem to advance, and make a space feel more closed-in. The same bedroom will seem intimate if it is decorated with warm colors, and open and expansive if it is decorated in cool hues.

The location of color in the bedroom will influence the style and character of the room. Dark or saturated colors placed low in the room will make the space feel defined and solid. Dark colors on the ceiling, however, may make the room seem claustrophobic; light colors on the ceiling will create the illusion of added height. Light-colored ceilings have the added benefit of reflecting more light into the room.

Designs or architecture with strong vertical patterns or lines will make a room appear smaller. If your bedroom has many tall, narrow windows, use the same color for the walls and draperies to make the space appear larger. Horizontal patterns or lines will visually enlarge an area. Wainscoting, for instance, draws attention to the total distance around the room, making it appear larger.

A variety of tones of the same color will keep a room from looking bland, and will help emphasize architecture and furnishings. But, if the architectural features or furnishings in the bedroom are disjointed to begin with, make textures the focus of interest and use colors of the same hue and value to unify the room.

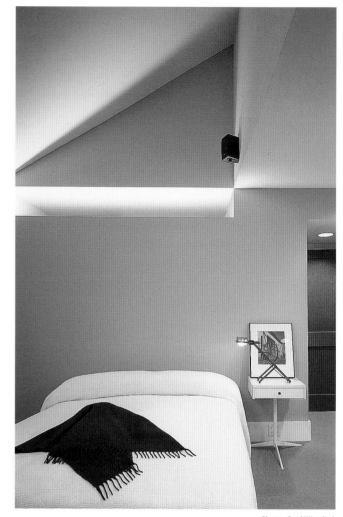

Photo: Paul Warchol

Use different colors on various planes and surfaces to enhance the geometry of architectural elements.

COLOR AND FUNCTION

When planning bedroom decor, consider the main uses of the room, then create an environment that supports the functional needs. If you use the bedroom almost exclusively for resting or sleeping, a tranquil palette may be most appropriate. If your definition of serenity is a meadow, start with pale grass greens and the soft colors of spring flowers. Or paint the ceiling the pastel of a peaceful sunset.

The bedroom also is for waking and dressing. Sunny yellow is a cheerful and radiant way to say "good morning world." Pristine white reflects light and gives the gentle energy needed to shake off sleep and speed you on your way.

For many, the bedroom is a romantic place. Delicious textures and warm colors suggest a sensuous, private retreat from the world. Beautiful bedroom palettes invite the inhabitants to spend time together there.

Bedrooms also are popular havens for studying or reading. Rich wood paneling, reminiscent of a library, may aid concentration. A few dashes of pure color—such as red—can add interest and focus to the room. Nurseries and juvenile bedrooms work well with bright, clear palettes of primary colors or primary colors and white.

This modern bedroom is no-nonsense when it comes to function, and its straightforward color scheme reflects a crisply efficient atmosphere.

Photo: Bedroom by Ligne Roset

COLOR AND STYLE

Each color, depending on its intensity and the hues adjacent to it, can be used to evoke many different moods and styles. People have measurable, physical responses to the vibration, energy, and light of color. For example, focusing on bright red will cause a rise in blood pressure. Pink, on the other hand, soothes people in stressful situations. And very large, unbroken areas of dark color can overpower the energy of some people, making them feel tired.

Although humans have immensely sophisticated color perception, simplicity and balance remain the most pleasing to the eye. Each part of a room's color palette has weight according to value, temperature, and excitement. Balance plays a role in each these factors.

Consider the value, or gray scale, of each color when developing a scheme. All colors have a corresponding gray value. For example, if you place a square of red, a square of sky blue, and a square of yellow side by side, and then take a black-and-white photograph of the arrangement, in the photo the red square will appear dark gray, the blue will be medium gray, and the yellow, very light gray. These are the gray values of the three colors. The middle value of gray, which is the midpoint between white and black, is perceived as the most restful value of gray.

Colors also should work together in terms of their *chroma*, a quality of color combining hue and saturation. Again, the key is balance: soft shades of lavender cool and balance bright yellow; green-blue will cool and balance a flaming hue of red; stark white can be tinted with a small amount of color to soften it without lessening its impact. A neutral bedroom color-scheme can be brought to life by adding a small area of pure color—much the way the petals of a flower brighten and enliven a forest or desert landscape.

Colors, of course, go in and out of style. Forecasting color trends is big business in the consumer and communication industries. The apparel industry most often sets the color trends, then the communications and interior design industries follow the fashion.

In many countries, the movement toward ecology has influenced color use. Green is newly popular, and often used as a neutral in color schemes—as it appears in nature. Recycled papers are making soft colors trendy—in packaging, stationary, and decor. Colors inspired by natural vegetable dyes are also becoming very popular in interior design.

At the same time that soft, natural colors are gaining popularity, the rise of international travel and the increase in production of goods in many countries are influencing palettes around the world. India and Central and South America have introduced us to the lavish use of pure colors juxtaposed in vivid patterns. Africa, the Middle East, and Indonesia have brought even more variety to our palettes, with contributions of bright batiks and the tones of henna and spices. And not a few sun-seeking travelers have developed cheerful bedroom palettes by emulating the bright pastels of stucco houses in the Mediterranean and Caribbean.

Last, as we have become more accustomed to bright colors, yellow has gained in popularity. It has long been traditional for traffic signs and vehicles because it stands out against other colors and in poor light. Advertisers now use it to increase the visibility of their products on the shelf. In cross-cultural word association studies, yellow consistently is linked with sunshine. It has made its way into interior design in the now popular hues of earthy orange, saffron, and sunflower.

*An isolated area of pure color
provides a vibrant focal point
in a bedroom of neutrals.*

Photo: E. Andrew McKinney
Design: Lou Ann Bauer Design

*This bedroom is an excellent example of
how complementary hues that are pure
and highly saturated will seem to vibrate
when placed side by side.*

THE NUTS AND BOLTS OF COLOR

 Every accomplished painter begins a work of art with a palette that determines the range of colors. A bedroom design can begin in a similar fashion; refining the harmony and balance of your chosen palette before you begin will help ensure good results. Here are a few tips for getting started.

If the colors you like are complementary colors—colors located on opposite sides of the color wheel—they will appear to vibrate when placed next to each other. The purer the colors, the greater the vibration. If your goal is to make the room tranquil, adding gray to the colors will slow their vibration. If your goal is just the opposite—the vibration becomes an advantage.

Remember that the size of the colored surface will affect your perception of the color. Some common-sense advice that has its roots in color theory: Colors appear stronger when they cover large areas than they do when they cover small areas. For instance, if the architecture of a room divides it into two different size areas, you can create the illusion of a single wall-color only if you paint the large expanses a slightly lighter tint of the color used in smaller areas.

Colors will also seem lighter or darker according to their adjacent colors. Red against a field of royal blue does not have nearly the power of red against a field of yellow. Thus, if you are using vibrant hues, take care to balance the supporting colors.

Photo: Bedroom by Brunschwig & Fils

The mix of checked, plaid, and floral prints in this bedroom work together because they share blue colors of the same value and saturation.

THE COLOR WHEEL

The colors you use in your bedroom make a personal statement. As you explore possible color combinations for your room, use the color wheel for guidance and inspiration. The color wheel shows the relationships among colors, and is an extremely helpful tool for manipulating colors successfully.

Photo: Bedroom by Cassina

The number of color schemes you can create for your bedroom is truly limitless.

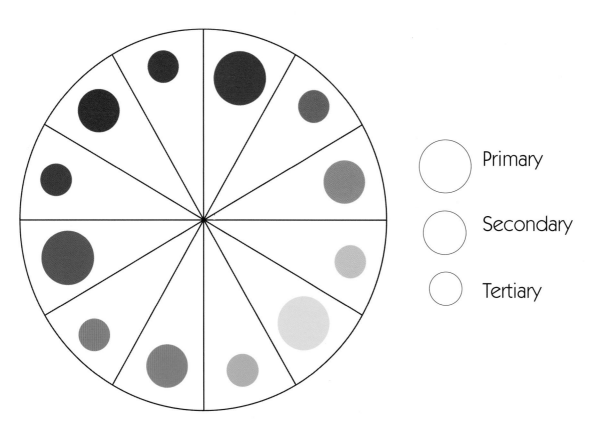

Primary

Secondary

Tertiary

COLOR THEORY

Color theory explains how colors relate to one another. The color wheel on page 22 presents colors in their logical sequence. Once you have decided on a base color, understanding color theory will give you a vocabulary of color with which to work.

Hue is the formal term for color, or color name, such as red, yellow, or blue. The relative lightness or darkness of a color is its *value*. Colors with white added are known as *tints*, and when black is added colors become *shades*. The intensity or brightness of a color is referred to as its degree of *saturation*, and *temperature* describes the perceived warmth or coolness of a color. Colors are combined in various ways to form *schemes*.

A *monochromatic* color scheme uses variations of one color, or only white, black, and gray in combination.

Monochromatic

Value Scale

Photo: Bedroom by Cassina

Analogous color schemes use three colors, or their tints and shades, which are next to each other on the color wheel. An analogous scheme might include red, red-orange, and yellow, or might consist of pink (which is a tint of red), red-orange, and yellow.

Analogous

A *complementary* color scheme employs colors from opposite sides of the color wheel—for example, purple and yellow.

Complementary

A *split complementary* scheme using the same example would pair purple with one of the two colors next to yellow on the wheel, either yellow-orange or yellow-green.

Split Complementary

A *triad* scheme uses three colors, or their shades or tints, that are equidistant on the color wheel, such as red, yellow, and blue.

Triad

Photo: Bedroom by Cassina

Combining pure colors such as red and yellow creates tremendous excitement in a room. Placing these colors next to white helps mute the vibration.

PURE COLORS
Colors with Intensity

The colors of gemstones, stained glass windows, and bright summer flowers—the mysterious intensity and excitement of these hues continues to inspire human beings to poetry and wanderlust. For those with the gusto to use pure colors in the bedroom, the results can be very rewarding.

Using two or more pure colors in the same room sets up a vivid vibration, making the colors seem to "jump." This effect is great in a nursery or room for children, but in bedrooms for adults more subtle schemes are usually desired. If you do choose to base your palette on a pure color, here are a few suggestions.

Palettes of pure colors work particularly well if one hue is used in the large areas and the others are used as accents. Or focus on a single pure color and pair it with a tint of itself or its complement. A hot red bedspread would electrify a mint green color scheme, but the color vibration would be held in check by the paleness of the green.

If you want to use lots of pure color—but don't want it to become overpowering—temper it with expanses of white or neutrals. Fabrics and wall-covering prints that combine intense colors with lots of white space work well with other solid areas of pure color. If a room is dominated by furniture or walls of dark wood, pure colors will brighten the space. Pairing black with a pure color scheme will increase the power of the colors—like turning up the volume on a stereo.

PURE COLORS PALETTE

Pure colors are the hues featured on the color wheel. They are the dominant point of each color wavelength, free from white or black, and they radiate high energy. The primary colors: blue, red, and yellow; the secondaries: purple, orange, and green; and all of the colors they create when combined are the clearest hues at your disposal. Paired with white, they become less obtrusive. Paired with black, they appear to come forward.

Cherry Red

Sunshine Yellow

Royal Blue

Purple

Orange Pepper

Emerald Green

Photo: Eric Roth

Bright yellow surfaces—like these walls—appear to advance toward the viewer. Accents of black and dark wood make yellow even more intense.

Cherry Red

Royal Blue

Warm White

Photo: David Livingston

Royal Blue

Cornflower

Cherry Red

Beach Sand

Around the windows, woodwork is painted white-tinted blue to harmonize the pure royal blue of the drapes with the sandy-colored neutrals in the walls and furniture. Extending around the room, a deep-blue cornice stripe emphasizes the sense of spaciousness in the room.

Three small, brightly colored geometric shapes add energy to this basic bedroom. The white walls and ceiling illustrate how a single color can unite an angular, divided space.

Photo: Peter Paige

Cherry Red

Royal Blue

Sunshine Yellow

The pure red, blue, and yellow of the bedspread and pillows work beautifully with the natural tints visible in the changing sky outside the room. The white stucco walls were kept bare to frame the view like a work of art.

Cherry Red

Mustard

Warm White

Here, red is teamed with white to enlarge the area. The energy of pure red—and the festive stripes, plaids, and floral patterns of the bed coverings and settee pillows—gives this room an extraordinarily warm atmosphere.

Photo: John Hall

Purple

Cherry Red

Royal Blue

Sunshine Yellow

Photo: Timothy Hursley

This contemporary bedroom takes its color inspiration from Bauhaus design. The warm hues of red, yellow, and golden-brown wood are balanced by cool blues and purple.

Delphinium

Terra Cotta

Warm White

Highly saturated blue on the walls and coffered ceiling creates drama, while white-painted trim and wainscoting bring more light to this large space.

Photo: Peter Paige

Orange Pepper

Persian Turquoise

Cherry Red

Purple

Emerald Green

Royal Blue

Intense, pure red makes a strong bedroom statement. Touches of complementary pure green keep the energy level high—so the cool teal, blue, purple, and gray hues elsewhere in the room balance and cool the scheme.

34

Photo: Emily Minton

Orange bedroom walls make for a warm, sunny start to the day. Balsam green, a close complement of orange, is shaded with black to keep the scheme from being too aggressively energetic.

Photo: David Livingston

El Sol

Warm White

Yellow walls and a coffered ceiling open up the space visually, and create an airy atmosphere for the large furniture. This bright and expansive hue of yellow reflects more light than most other colors.

Blueberry

Plum

Warm White

Unique color defines and shapes this striking bedroom. The walls are divided by color: saturated blue with upper panels of white to expand the space. The drapery panels alternate blue and white, adding a touch of whimsy to this very formal setting.

The complementary warmth of peach and the coolness of soft blue bring a felicitous balance to a lovely floral-striped bedroom.

TINTED COLORS
Colors for Tranquility

The soft colors of sunrise and sunset have a universal appeal. Whether in the colors of the dawn, greeting a glorious new day, or the colors of the sunset, signaling the end of our labors and return to the pleasures of home, pastel colors lift the spirit.

Pastel colors are tints: white mixed with a pure color to create a softer hue. Tints are among the easiest colors to harmonize, since they share a common element of white. Tints are also very soothing colors. The addition of white tones down even triad color schemes—such as red, yellow, and blue—that may look garish when used together at full strength. The more white is added to a color, the lower its vibration becomes.

In bedroom color schemes, it is best to use a range of pastel tints. Tints that are too close in value can make decor look boring instead of beautiful. You can avoid this by adding a touch of bright, saturated color to the room or by varying pale pastels with more vivid tints. Try adding touches of bright orange to a sherbet-pale peach decor. Or make a plain yellow and blue room exciting with creamy yellow walls and periwinkle blue fabrics.

Pastels are ideal for combining many prints and plaids for a richly layered effect. The softness of the colors lets the patterns stand out. In fact, the lighter the colors, the more they can be combined and manipulated—so you can splash away with many pastels with perfect confidence.

TINTED COLORS PALETTE

The tinted palette is a colorful rainbow of pastels. Cool and easy on the eye, soothing coral and pink, refreshing mint green and pale blue, and uplifting pale yellow bring calm cheer to any room.

Rosy Pink

Mint Green

Conch Pink

Light Yellow

Cerulean Blue

Spring Lavender

Photo: David Livingston

A palette of pastel tones can create the same serenity as a monochrome palette. Triad color schemes such as this one can make a pastel room be both peaceful and subtly energizing.

39

Bimini Blue

Cerulean Blue

Warm White

This clear blue bedroom makes a cool retreat from summer in the city. The ceiling is painted a slightly paler tint to give the small space a feeling of openness.

Photo: John Hall

Lemon Cream

Lemon Yellow

Blue Iris

Color is the main decorative feature in this room, with the fine detail of the graphic stripe adding interest to the large areas of flat color. This bedroom is an excellent example of how the creative use of paint can transform a simply furnished space.

Photo: Tim Street-Porter

Photo: Peter Paige

Cerulean Blue

The suggestion of a cloud-filled sky on the ceiling and bed cover gives this room a heavenly atmosphere. The cool blues are warmed by the beautiful natural wood.

Bimini Blue

Aqua

Moonlight Sand

Toast

Toast

Warm White

When viewed against a neutral background, tinted areas such as this aqua chair act as a focal point. While attention focuses on the most colorful feature in the room, the tint still is soft enough to avoid upstaging the artwork and unique furniture design.

Spring Lavender

Barely Blue

Golden Tan

The similar natural tan colors of the sisal rug and ceiling create the illusion that the pale blue walls are floating in between. The combination of cool and warm colors gives this bedroom a pleasant sense of energy.

Photo: David Livingston

Quiet tones of pale peach and camel create a tranquil bedroom and elegant backdrop for the beautiful stained glass windows. The beams and angled planes of the ceiling are lightly tinted, drawing attention to the architecture and creating a canopy that helps balance the visual weight of the carpet.

Peach Mist

Golden Glow

Soft Camel

Warm White

Iced Lilac

North Wind

When red-violet and blue-green are tinted to delicate, pale hues the effect is very cool and wistful.

Design: Luminae Souter Lighting Design

Butter Cream

A scheme that primarily consists of tints of one hue gains depth and character when shades of the same color are introduced.

Topaz

Soft White

Photo: Bedroom by Grange Furniture

Lavender Blue

Butter Cream

Blue and yellow—two time-honored companions—are nudged toward the unusual when the blue leans to lavender. The coolness of the wall-color works well in this room warmed by yellow fabrics, rich woods, and natural sunlight.

Photo: Steve Vierra

Barely Blue

Light Yellow

Rosy Pink

This triad scheme using tints of primary colors is a case study in color harmony. The values are relatively equal; no single color is more dominant than another. Because blue, yellow, and red are equidistant on the color wheel, this combination of tints is soothing but quietly enlivening as well.

Light Yellow

Warm White

This monochromatic color scheme is beautiful in its subtlety. The scheme benefits from the greens of plants and the outdoor landscape, which provide gentle contrast to the pale yellow tints.

Mint Julep

Moonlight Sand

Green, a secondary color, can be either warm or cool. This cool mint green evokes our association with living things and makes the room welcoming and restful. These green-sponged walls evoke a light-dappled meadow, with the sandy tans and deeper browns of the Oriental carpet adding to the sense of earthiness.

Photo: Steve Vierra

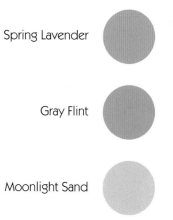

Spring Lavender

Gray Flint

Moonlight Sand

Mint

Light Yellow

Verdant Green

Blueberry

This color scheme and sleek contemporary furniture take their cues from a spring landscape. The saturated blue pillows on the bed are like a spray of hyacinth in a field of new grass.

Lavender picks up the soft gray in the room and highlights the architecture of the window, transforming its curved arc and rectangular panes into a clean-lined work of art.

Pink Frosting

Violet Blue

Spring Mint

Photo: Eric Roth

Conch Pink

Warm White

A single wall of color in a white room accentuates the geometry of the space. Here, peachy pink highlights the sinuous curves of the architecture.

When it comes to colors with reassuring, restful qualities, pink stands at the forefront. This bedroom captures the soft, feminine mood associated with the color.

Shaded colors bring high drama to a bedroom, but they drink in available light if they cover large areas. Putting a clear glaze on top of a dark wall increases light in the space by making the surface more reflective.

SHADED COLORS
Colors That Comfort

SHADED COLORS PALETTE

Warm colors are the cornerstone of this palette: rich red, golden yellow, mossy ocher green, the deep light-absorbing hues of the forest. The neutrals that work well with this palette tend to be warm rather than cool, although the sharp contrast of pure white often is introduced for its light-giving properties.

Chinese Red

Deep Blue

Deep Gold

Burnt Orange

Aubergine

Ocher Green

mages of days gone by and warm, cozy rooms with feather beds—shaded colors are perfect for creating an atmosphere of old-fashioned charm. The deep, rich quality of these darkened tones can make the bedroom a quiet, secure haven—a place to retreat from the fast pace of the outside world.

Shaded colors are created by adding black to a pure hue: Deep, rich, heavy colors are the result. The hot colors of summer become the pensive shades of autumn, shaded emerald becomes deep, forest green, and sapphire takes on the mystery of the ocean depths.

As with tints, shaded colors can be used in larger areas and combined more freely than pure colors. For example, a room painted with rich gold color has the sunny glow of a room painted yellow—but a much more restrained atmosphere. Accessorizing that room with deep crimson red and just a touch of pure cornflower blue creates a sophisticated palette of primary colors that is warm and full of energy.

The exclusive use of shaded hues in a bedroom creates a very intense space. Consider using white accents or perhaps a light tinted color to balance dark colors.

Photo: Frederick Charles

Large areas of taupe warm the cool blue colors in this bedroom. A metal wall sculpture and fireplace reflect light within the powerful expanse of the shaded inner walls.

Photo: Alan Weintraub

Ocher Green

Burnt Orange

The shaded green of this bedroom lounge area is complemented by the bed covering and mellow accents in deep reddish orange. The lighting and the natural woods of the ceiling and adjacent office space add further warmth.

Photo: Bedroom by Baker Furniture

Deep Gold

Balsam Green

Shaded hues always seem right with the wood and style of period furniture, perhaps because the upper classes of recent centuries made lavish use of color. White walls were unheard of in fine eighteenth-century homes.

Photo: David Livingston

Ripe Burgundy

Marble Gray

Barley

This bedroom illustrates how saturated color can successfully be incorporated into a room as long as light is a primary design consideration. The glass fireplace window lets in natural light, which is generously reflected by the pale neutral hues, white woodwork, and bed linens of the room.

Forest Green

Fathom Blue

White Linen

Bedrooms streaked with abundant sunlight are excellent candidates for a shaded palette. The deep value of the green walls gives an old world charm to this space, and the unexpected blue edging on the draperies and pillows adds a certain panache.

Photo: John Hall

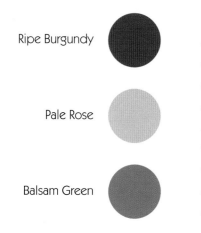

Ripe Burgundy

Pale Rose

Balsam Green

The repeating stripes of burgundy red and its rosy tint set a happy mood. The teal green horizontal stripe at the top of the walls balances the vertical stripes and keeps the room from appearing small.

Photo: Eric Roth

Soft White

Oatmeal

Dark Mahogany

Walls painted in a rich shade of bitter chocolate get a lift from brilliant white fabrics. Gathers and woven textures in the fabric give weight and dimension to the stark white.

Photo: Eric Roth

Chinese Red

Deep Gold

Green Pepper

Red and gold make this room blaze with the warmth of color. In keeping with the antique look, the faux-painted walls appear old and tarnished.

Design: Richard Reutlinger
Photo: Linda Svendsen

Deep Gold

Brown Maple

Chinese Red

With its exquisite woods, golden walls, and red accents, this room evokes the mood of a welcoming, glowing fire. Due to their powerful psychological associations, schemes of warm colors are ideal for cool, moist climates.

Aubergine

Peach Whisper

Monument Beige

No matter the time of day, this aubergine bedroom always offers the quiet, peaceful ambiance of night. Notice how critical the recessed ambient light is for the effective display of the artwork in such a dark space.

Deep Blue

Basil

Bone White

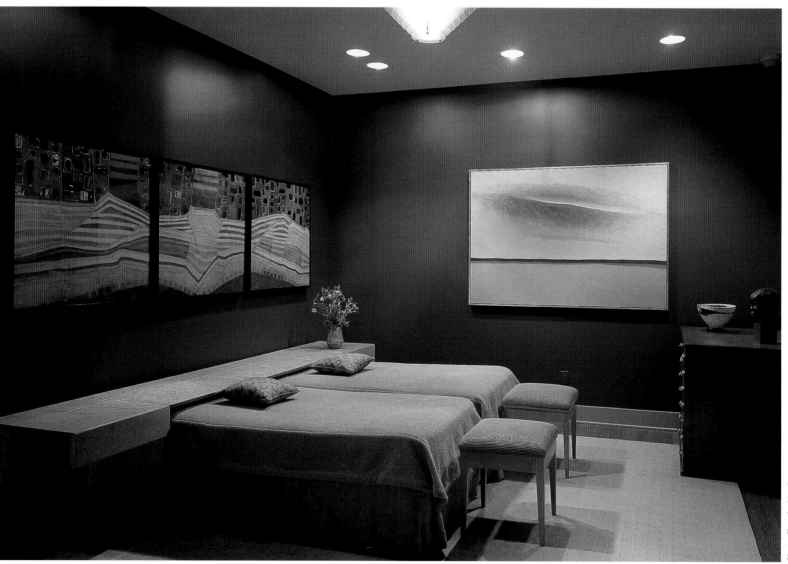

A *deep shade of blue envelops this collector's bedroom, providing a bold background for the eclectic style of art, artifacts, and fantasy sculpture. The lighter values of basil green and bone white accents provide relief and contrast.*

Photo: Balthazar Korab Ltd.

Two elements balance this room against the dramatic saturated red wall: The abundance of solid white gives off light, and the horizontal lines of the shoji screens increase the sense of spaciousness.

Photo: Steve Vierra

Toffee

Malted Milk

Chinese Red

When stripes are done in monochromatic colors—a shade with a tint, for instance—the effect is enlivening without being overwhelming. By accentuating architectural features, stripes can add quirky charm to a room.

Photo: Steve Vierra

Anasazi Red

Pecan Malt

Deep Blue

Peachy Rose

Bone White

Without the soft, complementary tones in the rug, the extremely dark color of these walls might seem harsh. Notice how the bedroom is outlined with a stripe where wall and ceiling meet—a technique many designers employ to keep shaded rooms from seeming smaller.

Photo: Eric Roth

Photo: Eric Roth

Nut Brown

Electric Blue

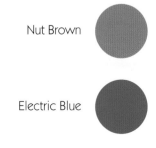

Artfully embracing the essential nature of this difficult space, the designer emphasized its closed-in feeling by painting the walls brown. A bold spiral pattern and slight gloss on the walls, along with vibrant blue in the bed linens and carpet, keep the mood exotic and exciting.

Muted schemes, such as this grayed complementary red and green palette, have unobtrusive, soothing personalities. Grayed tones strike just the right balance, respecting both the architecture and the people who live with the color scheme day in and day out.

MUTED COLORS
Colors for Easy Living

Muted colors are less saturated and lighter in value than pure colors. In bedroom decor, they engender a romantic, gentle ambiance—but have more solidity than pastels. In the muted palette, red becomes dusky rose, and blues, greens, and oranges become less intense, moving slightly toward gray without losing their identity. Muted palettes welcome occasional accents of more intense color.

Twilight Blue

Antique Rose

Willow Green

Dusky Peach

Harvest Grape

Copper Oxide Green

Muted palettes are versatile and easygoing—not too dark, too bright, too pale, or too colorless. For many people these hues are just right, particularly for the bedroom. To envision the palette, picture green leaves of willow trees seen through misty rain, reds and yellows of garden flowers softened by late dusk, and blue harbors filled with colorful boats beset by fog.

The softened muted colors are the result of graying, which can be achieved either by literally adding gray to a pure color or tint, or by mixing exact complements on the color wheel together to create a grayed effect. Many of the lighter-value muted colors have near-neutral status, in that the viewer sees them without necessarily consciously registering them as colors. Other grayed tones are more assertive, but their action still is nurturing and enveloping as opposed to demanding of attention.

The muted palette offers an array of moderate values that are good roommates over the long haul. They are ideal for the bedroom, eagerly responding to the light of morning and deepening after dark to match the hushed mood of night.

Photo: Steve Vierra

The reds in this room are muted with burnt orange but retain their vibrancy next to light walls painted in neutral taupe and cream. The horizontal line of the long, orange window-seat cushion balances the vertical lines of bed posts and striped walls.

Dusky Peach

Chardonnay

Harvest Grape

The tonal difference between the pale walls and slightly darker values of the casework enlarges this contemporary bedroom by making the walls seem to recede. Accents of purple bring additional interest to the space.

Photo: Luminae Souter
Design: James Benya

Bromeliad

Antique Rose

Brown Linen

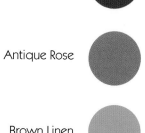

Lush muted red draperies and natural woodwork create a Victorian ambiance in this bedroom. The warm brown gives richness to the palette and eases the strength of the red.

Chinese Red

Tan Mushroom

*This bedroom is set
up to showcase the
artwork, with neu-
tral walls as a non-
interfering backdrop
and white on the
ceiling and trim to
allow for maximum
light. The rich rose
bedspread denotes a
cozy place to retreat.
Perhaps the palette
began with the rug.*

Photo: Michael Mundy

Lettuce Green

Faded Rose

Forest Green

Hibiscus Red

Complementary red and green—extremes of warm and cool— form the basis of this bedroom color scheme. The quilt vividly conveys the contrast.

Photo: Paul Warchol

Photo: Steven Brooke
Design: Dennis Jenkins

Gray Blue

Copper Oxide Green

Putty

Wrapping a room with the soft and inviting colors of nature is a good way to feature a fabulously unique work of art.

Antique Indigo

Toasty Orange

Silver Gray

The complementary scheme of gray-blue and orange brings cooling and warmth together, enriching the crisp contemporary furniture and art.

Photo: Warren Jagger

Willow Green

Red Berry

Shell Coral

Gray Blue

Dusky Peach

Willow Green

This charming bedroom shows how muted hues of the same value combine easily with one another, making it possible to use many different patterns on the furniture, walls, and bed coverings.

Nature-theme green wallpaper captures the spirit of the Arts and Crafts movement. This room has higher energy than many muted schemes, since the oak furniture glows golden and the complementary red pillows vibrate against the green walls.

Willow Green

Butter Cream

Warm White

Green walls with a soft gloss are kept light and cheerful by white bed linens and painted woodwork. Touches of yellow— from the same side of the color wheel as the warm green—add to the sunny ambiance.

Photo: Sam Gray

oto: Wardrobe by B&B Italia
sign: Studio Kairos

Rose Blush

Natural Buff

Parchment

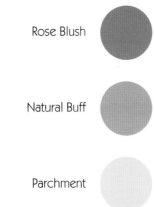

The rose tone of the wardrobe and head-board strikes a happy medium between blending with the neutral background and standing out as the color focal point. The wide parchment-gold stripe at the top of the far wall makes a gentle transition from the buff-colored panels to the bright white that rises to the ceiling.

Photo: Bedroom by Cassina

Twilight Blue

Tahitian Blue

Gravel Gray

This scheme is essentially monochromatic, but is stimulating to the eye because of the rich combination of dark blue, bright blue, and subtle gray. The solid colors give the sculptural lines of the contemporary furniture crisp definition.

Photo: Bedroom by Cassina

Chardonnay

Dusky Peach

Twilight Blue

Good color pairings can often be taken straight from nature. Here, peach and green bring a balance of warm and cool notes to a sunny room.

Neutral schemes are ideal for bringing artwork and the shapes and textures of furnishings into sharp relief. When planning a neutral color scheme for a bedroom, pay particular attention to sources of ambient and natural light, since the play of light and shadow is crucial to a successful design.

The Economics of Art Museums   Martin Feldstein

NEUTRAL COLORS
Colors of the Earth

The neutral palette evokes the serenity of the desert, pebbles and stones on a rocky beach, or bare trees and fields of grain during the last days of autumn. These subtle hues can create a bedroom that is the ultimate sophisticated retreat in the city or a soothing place to feel at peace in the countryside.

Any palette can be manipulated into an infinite variety of subtle neutral colors by mixing primary colors together or adding gray to neutralize a hue. The results are the browns, tans, beiges, taupes, and grays of the earth.

These are the colors that always remain in fashion. Neutral colors make a flattering backdrop for art objects and treasured pieces, showing forms, shapes, and colors to advantage. Wood, leather, and fibers can combine to make texture the partner of the neutral palette.

While a neutral tone-on-tone scheme can give a bedroom a very peaceful look, it also can easily cross the line to monotony and tedium. Here again, study the colors in nature—red blooms brightening the forest, bright shells on a sand beach—and add just a touch of color to make a neutral room come alive. Taking another cue from nature, emulate the drama of sunset by using ambient lighting to cause contrast and shadows.

Photo: Steven Brooke
Design: Dennis Jenkins

Unencumbered curved planes of pale color against the white ceiling flow with the suggestion of motion. The neutral color scheme is a perfect vehicle for expressing the varied textures in the room.

Photo: Paul Warchol

Soft Camel

Gunmetal Gray

Marble Gray

Soft tan and values of gray show off textures in this bedroom—stone, metal, sisal, and linen all come center stage. Notice how the red fabric, the lone bright color, stands out like a jewel in the sleek, uncluttered space.

Reddish Brown ●

Burnished Gold ●

Deep Blue ●

Buff ○

The neutral colors in this bedroom allow the historically authentic Chinese bed to dominate the room without interference. The reddish brown and deep grayish blue mimic the colors of traditional natural dyes.

Bone White

Gray Olive Green

Cameo Pink

Wheat

*Making all of the
vertical lines and
surfaces in this bed-
room the same
warm hue of white
unifies the space so
that it appears larg-
er. Gray tones in the
complementary red
and green accents
leave the tranquil
mood of the room
undisturbed.*

Photo: Steve Vierra

Photo: Tim Street-Porter

Wheat

Bone White

Bromeliad

The drama of this bedroom lies in the maple ceiling, whose golden wheat color draws attention to its unique, angled planes. Touches of red low in the room balance the visual weight of the ceiling, while pale, bone white brings the color scheme together without conflict.

Photo: Steve Whittaker

Putty

Peach

Sponged walls, a loosely woven throw, pillows with a metallic glow, and smooth-surfaced night tables—these textures become all the more sensuous in a neutral scheme. A muted-peach duvet cover adds color without disturbing the mood.

White Linen

Gray Verdigris

Gray Olive Green

A pure sweep of white-on-white readily suggests luxury and elegance, and this bedroom is no exception. Spare touches of dark hues high and low in the room keep the space from looking sterile.

Photo: Steve Rosenthal

White Linen

Soft Camel

Dark Mahogany

Ebony

Pale vertical stripes on the wall and in the bed covering contrast with the dark colors and horizontal lines of the bookcases and doors. The pottery collection adds a refreshing touch of color to this neutral palette.

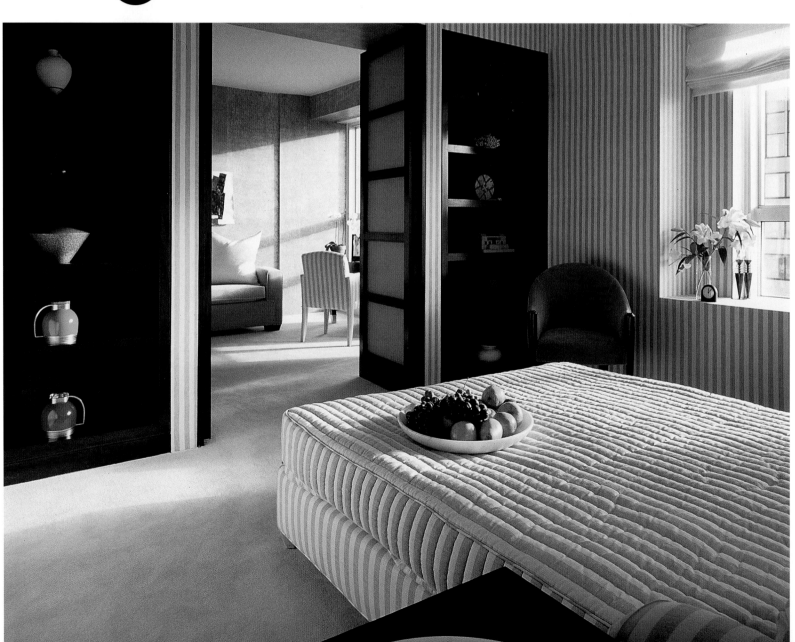

Photo: Tim Street-Porter

Gunmetal Gray

Parchment

White Linen

Translucent gray makes the sleeping area in this bedroom softer than its high-tech surroundings. The natural palette shows off the fascinating design and unique shape of the bed.

Bone White

Driftwood

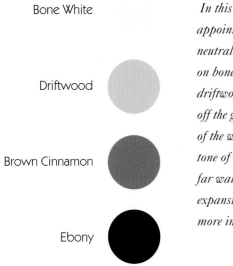

Brown Cinnamon

Ebony

In this beautifully appointed room, a neutral scheme built on bone-white and driftwood tan shows off the glowing finish of the wood. A warm tone of brown on the far wall makes the expansive room seem more intimate.

Gray Marble

Cane

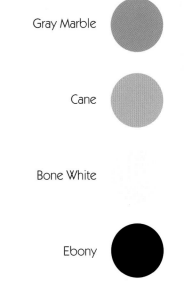

Bone White

Ebony

An urban bedroom illustrates how light is an integral piece of the design story in a neutral space. Note the cove lighting high at the arc of the far wall, the bright green of the bedside lamps, and the natural light that is reflected above the bed.

Photo: Richard Mandelkorn

Bleached Taupe

Flax

Natural Wood

Pale colors get a boost from the gilded surfaces of furniture and the metallic sheen of drapery and upholstery fabrics. The resulting glow of ambient light quietly enlivens this subtle, restful palette.

Bone White

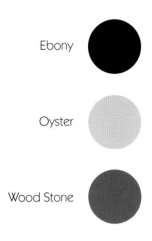

Ebony

Oyster

Wood Stone

When the ceiling of a room is dark, it is tempting to go too far toward white to lighten the room. Here, black furniture and doors stand out in sharp relief in an oyster white bedroom, balancing the dark wood ceiling.

Photo: Richard Mandelkorn

99

Bone White

Orange Clay

Ebony

Multiple hues of soft white draw attention toward graphic accents of black and orange. Note how the light color makes the interesting architectural elements stand out clearly.

Photo: Wade Zimmerman

Bone White

Parchment

Brown Earth

Ebony

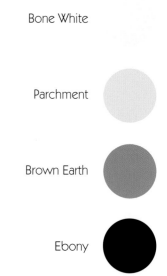

Metallic mixes well with the neutral palette, and can work as an accent or dark color in a neutral scheme. Here, the mottled white and gold finish on the walls creates a textured look well suited to the safari styling and zebra accent rug in this bedroom.

Bone White

Gray Olive Green

Many designers turn to an all-white scheme as a low-key background for collections of decorative objects. The simplicity of the palette in this bedroom is matched by the minimalist furnishings, resulting in unsurpassed, sheer elegance.

Photo: Eric Roth

Stone

Driftwood

Oyster

A scheme of taupes and grays holds together the design of this eclectic room, where the textures range from rough to smooth and the furnishings from contemporary to traditional. A bouquet of red roses in a shiny metal pail adds the requisite dash of color.

Choosing a different color for every curtain panel makes a flashy design statement in and of itself, but when the hues are bright orange, pink, and green, the message clearly is hot, hot, hot.

ELECTRIC COLORS
Colors with Energy

ELECTRIC COLORS PALETTE

The electric look can be achieved by using pure, saturated colors with intensity. Place complementary colors next to each other to heighten their contrast. Or use strong contrast like Moroccan red against sunburst yellow to light up a bedroom. Pairing black and white geometric shapes with these bright colors is very stimulating.

Moroccan Red

Sunburst Yellow

Hot Plum

Ocean Blue

Persimmon Orange

Bright Chartreuse

Sizzle Pink

Neon signs, computer screens, and animated electronic games—electric colors cover the full spectrum of wild, clashing colors. The age of information has ushered in a whole new visual world: Packaging, magazines, direct mail, and advertising all come in outrageous color combinations created to grab our attention.

Interior design is always influenced by the style of the day, so it comes as no surprise that the high energy and high-tech spirit of the era is reflected in living spaces—even in the bedroom. Granted, bedrooms emblazoned with electric colors are not for everyone. But for some, an intense color palette offers energy at the beginning and end of each day. These bedroom color schemes encourage a no-holds-barred attitude toward life.

Using Day-Glo hues—which appear to be lit from within—will strengthen the impact of unexpected and clashing color schemes. Another route to the electric is to manipulate the palette. You can create visual high energy with strong opposites, pairing such colors as hot magenta and lime green.

Any color placed next to black or with black and white will become more intense. Using black and white in checks or stripes is very exciting to the eye, as is the use of colors in bold, geometric shapes.

Photo: John Hall

On large surfaces, electric colors appear more intense and seem to glow. They are the ultimate attention-getters, boldly accentuating the lines and shapes of architecture in the bedroom. To get colors this saturated, you must use pigment-based paints rather than chalk-based ones.

Moroccan Red

Goldenrod

Sycamore

Color in this bedroom is a modern interpretation of a Rembrandt painting. The muted gold and green in the tapestry hearken back to a bygone era, while the bold red fabric draws attention to the contemporary architecture. The red vertical line is a counterpoint to the dark horizontal beams.

Photo: Tim Street-Porter

Sunburst Yellow

Crimson Red

Blue Velvet

Emerald Green

The electricity in this bedroom is created by the energy of highly saturated complementary colors. Gold leaf on the intricate carving increases the effect of light bouncing out toward the viewer.

Ocean Blue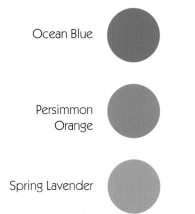

Persimmon Orange

Spring Lavender

Complementary blue and orange are the basis of this vibrant color scheme. Using several values of cool blue tones accented with yellows and oranges increases the drama in any bedroom.

Photo: Steven Brooke
Design: Dennis Jenkins

Photo: Steven Brooke
Design: Dennis Jenkins

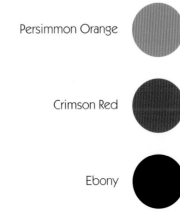

Persimmon Orange

Crimson Red

Ebony

Black against white always sets up vibration, and the repetition of checked patterns strengthens the effect. Place check-patterns next to bright orange and red, and you have a bedroom that is for the young at heart, but certainly not for the faint of heart.

Photo: Tim Street-Porter

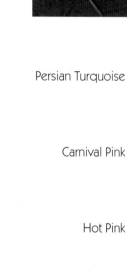

Persian Turquoise

Carnival Pink

Hot Pink

Slate Blue

The tinted pink and turquoise wall colors are extra intense, with no black or gray mixed in the paint. The ebony horizontal line around the room creates contrast that makes the colors seem even more vivid.

Hot Plum

Purple Ice

Sandy Buff

The purple and buff ceiling of this room is integral to the design, since it mirrors in color the rhythm of the furnishings below. Flowing bed curtains tie the room together in an intimate gesture—softening the theatrical impact of the space.

Photo: Norman McGrath

Photo: Norman McGrath

Bright Plum

Electric Purple

Shaded Purple

Purple and plum fabrics ignite the mood in this bedroom. Indirect lighting creates interesting surface contrasts and cool, white walls add to the aura of sophistication.

Purple Mist

Regency Blue

Chanel Red

Lemon Yellow

Seal Gray

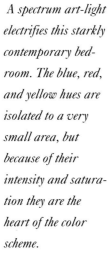

*A **spectrum art-light** electrifies this starkly contemporary bedroom. The blue, red, and yellow hues are isolated to a very small area, but because of their intensity and saturation they are the heart of the color scheme.*

Photo: Norman McGrath

Bright Chartreuse

Daffodil Yellow

Persimmon Orange

Holly Berry Red

Day-Glo colors give this room neon brilliance. A touch of silver gray and wooden floors are the only influences that cool things down a bit, but shiny surfaces keep the energy sky-high.

COLOR SWATCHES

Color swatches can help you pinpoint the colors you find most appealing. Clip the swatches provided here and use them to create color schemes of your own design. The following colors appear in "rainbow" order—according to their arrangement in the color spectrum. Turn to the page numbers indicated to see the colors featured in a bedroom design.

Lemon Yellow PAGE 41, 112	**Daffodil Yellow** PAGE 113	**White Linen** PAGE 61, 93, 94, 95	**Goldenrod** PAGE 106	**Wheat** PAGE 90, 91	**Wood Stone** PAGE 99
Lemon Cream PAGE 41	**Butter Cream** PAGE 47, 48, 82	**Toffee** PAGE 69	**Topaz** PAGE 47	**Flax** PAGE 98	**Brown Maple** PAGE 65
Soft White PAGE 47, 63	**Buff** PAGE 89	**Mustard** PAGE 31	**Beach Sand** PAGE 28	**Orange Pepper** PAGE 34	**Soft Camel** PAGE 44, 88, 94
Malted Milk PAGE 69	**Light Yellow** PAGE 49, 50, 52	**Burnished Gold** PAGE 89	**Golden Tan** PAGE 44	**Natural Wood** PAGE 98	**Tan Mushroom** PAGE 76
Sunburst Yellow PAGE 106	**Bone White** PAGE 66, 70, 90, 91, 96, 99, 100, 102	**Parchment** PAGE 83, 95, 100	**Pecan Malt** PAGE 69	**Cane** PAGE 96	**Peach Mist** PAGE 44
Sunshine Yellow PAGE 30, 32	**Bleached Taupe** PAGE 98	**Deep Gold** PAGE 59, 64, 65	**Sandy Buff** PAGE 111	**Barley** PAGE 60	**Brown Cinnamon** PAGE 96
El Sol PAGE 36	**Golden Glow** PAGE 44	**Warm White** PAGE 28, 31, 33, 36, 40, 42, 44, 50, 54, 82	**Monument Beige** PAGE 66	**Nut Brown** PAGE 71	**Driftwood** PAGE 96, 102

Wood Stone PAGE 99	**Wheat** PAGE 90, 91	**Goldenrod** PAGE 106	**White Linen** PAGE 61, 93, 94, 95	**Daffodil Yellow** PAGE 113	**Lemon Yellow** PAGE 41, 112
Brown Maple PAGE 65	**Flax** PAGE 98	**Topaz** PAGE 47	**Toffee** PAGE 69	**Butter Cream** PAGE 47, 48, 82	**Lemon Cream** PAGE 41
Soft Camel PAGE 44, 88, 94	**Orange Pepper** PAGE 34	**Beach Sand** PAGE 28	**Mustard** PAGE 31	**Buff** PAGE 89	**Soft White** PAGE 47, 63
Tan Mushroom PAGE 76	**Natural Wood** PAGE 98	**Golden Tan** PAGE 44	**Burnished Gold** PAGE 89	**Light Yellow** PAGE 49, 50, 52	**Malted Milk** PAGE 69
Peach Mist PAGE 44	**Cane** PAGE 96	**Pecan Malt** PAGE 69	**Parchment** PAGE 83, 95, 100	**Bone White** PAGE 66, 70, 90, 91, 96, 99, 100, 102	**Sunburst Yellow** PAGE 106
Brown Cinnamon PAGE 96	**Barley** PAGE 60	**Sandy Buff** PAGE 111	**Deep Gold** PAGE 59, 64, 65	**Bleached Taupe** PAGE 98	**Sunshine Yellow** PAGE 30, 32
Driftwood PAGE 96, 102	**Nut Brown** PAGE 71	**Monument Beige** PAGE 66	**Warm White** PAGE 28, 31, 33, 36, 40, 42, 44, 50, 54, 82	**Golden Glow** PAGE 44	**El Sol** PAGE 36

Toasty Orange PAGE 79	**Chanel Red** PAGE 112	**Reddish Brown** PAGE 89	**Moroccan Red** PAGE 106	**Ripe Burgundy** PAGE 60, 62	**Carnival Pink** PAGE 110
Shell Coral PAGE 80	**Terra Cotta** PAGE 33	**Crimson Red** PAGE 106, 109	**Peachy Rose** PAGE 70	**Antique Rose** PAGE 74	**Hot Plum** PAGE 111
Burnt Orange PAGE 58	**Dusky Peach** PAGE 74, 80, 85	**Conch Pink** PAGE 54	**Peach Whisper** PAGE 66	**Rosy Pink** PAGE 49	**Bright Plum** PAGE 112
Natural Buff PAGE 83	**Peach** PAGE 92	**Cherry Red** PAGE 28, 30, 31, 32, 34	**Chinese Red** PAGE 64, 65, 69, 76	**Pink Frosting** PAGE 54	**Plum** PAGE 36
Persimmon Orange PAGE 108, 109, 113	**Chardonnay** PAGE 74, 85	**Cameo Pink** PAGE 90	**Pale Rose** PAGE 62	**Red Berry** PAGE 80	**Aubergine** PAGE 66
Brown Linen PAGE 74	**Orange Clay** PAGE 100	**Faded Rose** PAGE 77	**Bromeliad** PAGE 74, 91	**Hot Pink** PAGE 110	**Purple Ice** PAGE 111
Holly Berry Red PAGE 113	**Anasazi Red** PAGE 69	**Rose Blush** PAGE 83	**Hibiscus Red** PAGE 77	**Iced Lilac** PAGE 46	**Electric Purple** PAGE 112

Carnival Pink PAGE 110	Ripe Burgundy PAGE 60, 62	Moroccan Red PAGE 106	Reddish Brown PAGE 89	Chanel Red PAGE 112	Toasty Orange PAGE 79
Hot Plum PAGE 111	Antique Rose PAGE 74	Peachy Rose PAGE 70	Crimson Red PAGE 106, 109	Terra Cotta PAGE 33	Shell Coral PAGE 80
Bright Plum PAGE 112	Rosy Pink PAGE 49	Peach Whisper PAGE 66	Conch Pink PAGE 54	Dusky Peach PAGE 74, 80, 85	Burnt Orange PAGE 58
Plum PAGE 36	Pink Frosting PAGE 54	Chinese Red PAGE 64, 65, 69, 76	Cherry Red PAGE 28, 30, 31, 32, 34	Peach PAGE 92	Natural Buff PAGE 83
Aubergine PAGE 66	Red Berry PAGE 80	Pale Rose PAGE 62	Cameo Pink PAGE 90	Chardonnay PAGE 74, 85	Persimmon Orange PAGE 108, 109, 113
Purple Ice PAGE 111	Hot Pink PAGE 110	Bromeliad PAGE 74, 91	Faded Rose PAGE 77	Orange Clay PAGE 100	Brown Linen PAGE 74
Electric Purple PAGE 112	Iced Lilac PAGE 46	Hibiscus Red PAGE 77	Rose Blush PAGE 83	Anasazi Red PAGE 69	Holly Berry Red PAGE 113

Purple Mist PAGE 112	**Violet Blue** PAGE 54	**Electric Blue** PAGE 71	**Ocean Blue** PAGE 108	**Aqua** PAGE 42	**Emerald Green** PAGE 34, 106
Purple PAGE 32, 34	**Shaded Purple** PAGE 112	**Regency Blue** PAGE 112	**Blue Velvet** PAGE 106	**Copper Oxide Green** PAGE 78	**Lettuce Green** PAGE 77
Spring Lavender PAGE 44, 52, 108	**Deep Blue** PAGE 66, 70, 89	**Slate Blue** PAGE 110	**Antique Indigo** PAGE 79	**PersianTurquoise** PAGE 34, 110	**Mint Julep** PAGE 51
Harvest Grape PAGE 74	**Gray Blue** PAGE 78, 80	**Blue Iris** PAGE 41	**Tahitian Blue** PAGE 84	**Spring Mint** PAGE 54	**Green Pepper** PAGE 64
Lavender Blue PAGE 48	**Gray Flint** PAGE 52	**Barely Blue** PAGE 44, 49	**Bimini Blue** PAGE 40, 42	**Forest Green** PAGE 61, 77	**Verdant Green** PAGE 52
Royal Blue PAGE 28, 30, 32, 34	**Delphinium** PAGE 33	**Twilight Blue** PAGE 84, 85	**Cerulean Blue** PAGE 40, 42	**Gray Verdigris** PAGE 93	**Mint** PAGE 52
Blueberry PAGE 36, 52	**Cornflower** PAGE 28	**Fathom Blue** PAGE 61	**North Wind** PAGE 46	**Balsam Green** PAGE 59, 62	**Sycamore** PAGE 106

Emerald Green PAGE 34, 106	**Aqua** PAGE 42	**Ocean Blue** PAGE 108	**Electric Blue** PAGE 71	**Violet Blue** PAGE 54	**Purple Mist** PAGE 112
Lettuce Green PAGE 77	**Copper Oxide Green** PAGE 78	**Blue Velvet** PAGE 106	**Regency Blue** PAGE 112	**Shaded Purple** PAGE 112	**Purple** PAGE 32, 34
Mint Julep PAGE 51	**PersianTurquoise** PAGE 34, 110	**Antique Indigo** PAGE 79	**Slate Blue** PAGE 110	**Deep Blue** PAGE 66, 70, 89	**Spring Lavender** PAGE 44, 52, 108
Green Pepper PAGE 64	**Spring Mint** PAGE 54	**Tahitian Blue** PAGE 84	**Blue Iris** PAGE 41	**Gray Blue** PAGE 78, 80	**Harvest Grape** PAGE 74
Verdant Green PAGE 52	**Forest Green** PAGE 61, 77	**Bimini Blue** PAGE 40, 42	**Barely Blue** PAGE 44, 49	**Gray Flint** PAGE 52	**Lavender Blue** PAGE 48
Mint PAGE 52	**Gray Verdigris** PAGE 93	**Cerulean Blue** PAGE 40, 42	**Twilight Blue** PAGE 84, 85	**Delphinium** PAGE 33	**Royal Blue** PAGE 28, 30, 32, 34
Sycamore PAGE 106	**Balsam Green** PAGE 59, 62	**North Wind** PAGE 46	**Fathom Blue** PAGE 61	**Cornflower** PAGE 28	**Blueberry** PAGE 36, 52

COLOR GLOSSARY

Analogous Color Scheme — A scheme that uses three colors (or their tints and shades) that are next to each other on the color wheel.

Chroma — Chroma is the degree of brilliance of a color.

Complementary Color Scheme — A color scheme that uses colors from opposite sides of the color wheel.

Hue — Hue is the formal term for color.

Monochromatic Color Scheme — A color scheme that uses only variations of one color, or a scheme that uses only white, black, and gray.

Saturation — Saturation is the intensity or brightness of a color.

Shades — Shades (or dark values) are colors with black added to them.

Split Complementary Scheme — A color scheme made up of any color combined with two colors on either side of its complement on the color wheel.

Temperature — The perceived warmth or coolness of a color.

Tints — Tints (or light tonal values) are colors with white added to them.

Triad Color Scheme — A color scheme that uses three colors (or their tints or shades) that are equidistant on the color wheel.

Value — Value (or tonal value) is the relative lightness or darkness of a color.

Willow Green	Ocher Green	Toast
PAGE 80, 82	PAGE 58	PAGE 42
Basil	Bright Chartreuse	Brown Earth
PAGE 66	PAGE 113	PAGE 100
Gray Olive Green	Marble Gray	Dark Mahogany
PAGE 90, 93, 102	PAGE 60, 88	PAGE 63, 94
Ebony	Seal Gray	Putty
PAGE 94, 96, 99, 100, 109	PAGE 112	PAGE 78, 92
Gunmetal Gray	Gravel Gray	Oyster
PAGE 88, 95	PAGE 84	PAGE 99, 102
Stone	Silver Gray	Oatmeal
PAGE 102	PAGE 79	PAGE 63
Gray Marble	Moonlight Sand	Black
PAGE 96	PAGE 42, 51, 52	

Toast PAGE 42	Ocher Green PAGE 58	Willow Green PAGE 80, 82
Brown Earth PAGE 100	Bright Chartreuse PAGE 113	Basil PAGE 66
Dark Mahogany PAGE 63, 94	Marble Gray PAGE 60, 88	Gray Olive Green PAGE 90, 93, 102
Putty PAGE 78, 92	Seal Gray PAGE 112	Ebony PAGE 94, 96, 99, 100, 109
Oyster PAGE 99, 102	Gravel Gray PAGE 84	Gunmetal Gray PAGE 88, 95
Oatmeal PAGE 63	Silver Gray PAGE 79	Stone PAGE 102
Black	Moonlight Sand PAGE 42, 51, 52	Gray Marble PAGE 96

INDEX

B&B Italia 6, 83

Baker Furniture 15, 59

Balthazar Korab, Ltd. 67, 79

Benya, James 74

Bordwin, Andrew 27

Brooke, Steven 78, 87, 108, 109

Brunschwig & Fils 20, 38

Cassina 1, 13, 22, 23, 24, 25, 84, 85

Charles, Frederick 43, 57

Crate & Barrel 35

Dakota Jackson 14, 52

Grange Furniture 48

Gray, Sam 82, 86

Grove, Jim 123

Hales, Mick 8, 63

Hall, John 31, 40, 61, 75, 104, 114

Hursley, Timothy 32, 66

Jagger, Warren 53, 80

Jenkins, Dennis 78, 87, 108, 109

Joseph W. Drohan Associates 4

Karosis, Rob 81, 103, 105

Kaufman, Elliott 94

Ligne Roset 17

Livingston, David 28, 36, 39, 44, 60, 101

Luminae Souter Lighting Design 46, 74, 96

Mandelkorn, Richard 98, 99

McGrath, Norman 111, 112

McKinney, E. Andrew 21

Minton, Emily 34

Mundy, Michael 10, 37, 76

Paige, Peter 30, 33, 42, 47

Reutlinger, Richard 65

Rosenthal, Steve 93

Roth, Eric 4, 27, 54, 56, 62, 64, 70, 71, 72, 102

Street-Porter, Tim 41, 89, 91, 95, 106, 107, 110

Studio Kairos 83

Svendsen, Linda 65

Vierra, Steve 49, 68, 69, 73, 90

Warchol, Paul 16, 19, 29, 45, 77, 88, 97, 113

Weintraub, Alan 58

Whittaker, Steve 92

Zimmerman, Wade 100

DIRECTORY OF PHOTOGRAPHERS

Andrew Bordwin
70 A Greenwich Avenue #332
New York, NY 10011

Steven Brooke
7910 SW 54 Court
Miami, FL 33143

Frederick Charles
254 Park Avenue South
New York, NY 10010

Sam Gray
23 Westwood Road
Wellesley, MA 02181

Jim Grove
One Mono Lane
San Anselmo, CA 94960

Mick Hales
Green World Pictures, Inc.
North Richardsville Road, RD #2
Carmel, NY 10512

John Hall
John Hall Photographs
500 West 58th #3F
New York, NY 10019

Timothy Hursley
1911 West Markham
Little Rock, AR 72205

Warren Jagger
150 Chestnut Street
Providence, RI 02903

Dennis Jenkins
5813 SW 68th Street
South Miami, FL 33143

Rob Karosis
855 Islington
Portsmouth, NH 03801

Elliott Kaufman
255 West 90th Street #5L
New York, NY 10024

Balthazar Korab
5051 Beach Road
Troy, MI 48098

David Livingston
1036 Erica Road
Mill Valley, CA 94941

Richard Mandelkorn
65 Beaver Pond Road
Lincoln, MA 01773

Norman McGrath
164 West 79th Street
New York, NY 10024

E. Andrew McKinney
180 1/2 Tenth Avenue
San Francisco, CA 94118

Emily Minton
3004 13th Avenue South #1
Birmingham, AL 35205

Michael Mundy
25 Mercer Street
New York, NY 10013

Peter Paige
269 Parkside Road
Harrington Park, ND 07640

Steve Rosenthal
59 Maple Street
Auburndale, MA 02116

Eric Roth
337 Summer Street
Boston, MA 02210

Tim Street-Porter
2074 Watsonia Terrace
Los Angeles, CA 90068

Linda Svendsen
3915 Bayview Circle
Concord, CA 94520

Steve Vierra
P.O. Box 1827
Sandwich, MA 02563

Paul Warchol
133 Mulberry Street
New York, NY 10013

Alan Weintraub
1832A Mason Street
San Francisco, CA 94133

Steve Whittaker
1155 Chess Drive
Suite 125
Foster City, CA 94404

Wade Zimmerman
9 East 97th Street
New York, NY 10029

DIRECTORY OF ARCHITECTS/DESIGNERS/MANUFACTURERS

Charlene Allen and
Joan D'Ambrosia
Beautiful Things, Beautiful
Interiors
43 Bacon Lane
Centerville, MA 02632

Julie Alvarez de Toledo
No. 2 off Forest Street
Manchester, MA 01944

Auberge St. Antoine
10 rue St. Antoine
Quebec, Quebec G1K 4C9
Canada

B&B Italia, USA, Inc.
150 East 58 Street
Architects and Designers
Building
New York, NY 10155

Baker Furniture
1661 Monroe Avenue, N.W.
Grand Rapids, MI 49505

Clara Hayes Barrett
300 Boylston Street
Boston, MA 02116

Bierly-Drake Associates Inc.
17 Arlington Street
Boston, MA 02116

Brunschwig & Fils
979 Third Avenue
New York, NY 10022

Captain Lord Mansion
P.O. Box 800
Kennebunkport, ME 04046

Cassina USA
200 McKay Road
Huntington Station, NY 11746

Celeste Cooper, ASID
Repetoire
560 Harrison Avenue
Boston, MA 02118

Crate & Barrel
For information and the
 nearest store, call
(800) 451-8217

Dakota Jackson, Inc.
42-24 Orchard Street
Long Island City, NY 11101

Joseph W. Drohan Associates
One Sprucewood Avenue
Nashua, NH 03062

Marian Glasgow
9 Laurel Street
Newton Centre, MA 02159

Grange Furniture Inc.
New York Design Center
200 Lexington Avenue
New York, NY 10016

Carole Kaplan, ASID
Two By Two Interior Design Ltd.
34 School Street
Andover, MA 01810

Ligne Roset
Roset USA Corporation
200 Lexington Avenue
New York, NY 10016

Veronique Louvet
66 Haskell Street
Beverly Farms, MA 01915

Luminae-Souter Lighting Design
1740 Army Street, 2nd Floor
San Francisco, CA 94125

Delight Nelson
Interiors Delight
17 Cadagon Way
Nashua, NH 03062

Pomegranate Inn
49 Neal Street
Portland, ME 04102

Andrew Reczkowski
102 Watts Street
Chelsea, MA 02150

Nancy Reynolds and Thomas
Wineman
11 Oak Lane
Osterville, MA 02655

Roycroft Inn
40 South Grove Street
East Aurora, NY 14052

Michael Tovano
Onavet
16 Randolph Street
P.O. Box 1170
Boston, MA 02117

Stephen Tucker, AIA
144 Lincoln Street
Boston, MA 02111

Gary Wolf, AIA
Gary Wolf Architects, Inc.
145 Hanover Street
Boston, MA 02108

BIBLIOGRAPHY

Birren, Faber. *Munsell, A Grammar of Color.* New York: Van Nostrand Reinhold, 1969.

Birren, Faber. *Principles of Color.* New York: Van Nostrand Reinhold, 1969.

Birren, Faber. *The Story of Color.* Westport, CT: The Crimson Press, 1941.

Graham, F. Lanier. *The Rainbow Book.* New York: Vintage Books, 1979.

Kobayashi, Shigenobu. *A Book of Colors.* New York: Harper and Row, Publishers, Inc, 1987.

Levinson, Henry W. *Artists' Pigments.* Hallandale, FL: COLORLAB,1976.

Luckiesh, Matthew. *Language of Color.* New York: Dodd, Mead and Company, 1918.

May, Rollo. *My Quest for Beauty.* Dallas, TX: Saybrook Publishing Company, 1985.

Robinson, Stuart. *A History of Printed Textiles.* Cambridge: M.I.T. Press, 1971.

Telford, Anne. "Color Predictions." *Communication Arts*, vol. 34, no. 8 (January/February 1993), pp. 70–73.

Telford, Anne. "Color Predictions." *Communication Arts*, vol. 35, no. 8 (January/February 1994), pp. 90–95.

Thomas, Anne Wall. *Colors from the Earth.* New York: Van Nostrand Reinhold, 1980.

Wilcox, Michael. *Blue and Yellow Don't Make Green.* Rockport, MA: Rockport Publishers, 1989.